COPYRIGHT © 2023
St Shenouda Press

All rights reserved. No part of this book may be reproduced in any manner without prior written permission from the publisher.

Book Design: Sandra Bottros
Editor: Kirollos Nassief

ST SHENOUDA PRESS
8419 Putty Rd,
Putty, NSW, 2330
Sydney, Australia

www.stshenoudapress.com

ISBN: 978-0-6457704-1-4

Scan the QR code to go to our website where you will find

- Book reviews

- Great deals

- Our full library of books

My parents were devout Christians who loved God very much. My mother, Euphemia, was barren however, and so could not have children. My parents were upset by this, and so spent long hours praying and fasting, asking God to grant them a child. At the time of the feast of St Mary, my mother stood in front of the icon of St Mary and asked her for a son. While she was speaking to St Mary, she heard the word "Amen" coming from the icon. That confirmed to my mother that she would have a boy in response to her prayers.

In 285 AD in Egypt, my mother gave birth and named the boy Mena, which comes from "Amen". God also gave my parents a baby girl two years later – me!
My parents frequently read the Holy Bible with us and taught us the traditions of the Coptic Church. My brother and I enjoyed going to church more than anywhere else. Mena especially loved to talk with God through prayer. I would see him praying in the morning, throughout the day and at night before bedtime too.

Our father Eudoxius died when Mena was 14 years old. I was almost 12 at the time. A little later, my mother also passed away. This was very distressing for us, but the Lord comforted and took care of us. Following what our parents taught us about the love of Christ, my brother and I took the wealth that we inherited from them and gave it away to the poor. Helping other people in need was our true joy. A year later, the region's new governor, who was a friend of our father, talked Mena into joining the Roman army.

Since our father was also a ruler, he was given a high rank in the army. He went to Nigeria to serve there for three years. I missed him very much but knew that serving in the army was something that he really wanted to do.

Mena made many friends there and was loved by all. They admired how he always thought of others before himself. Despite being in a different country, he continued to be a strong Christian, preaching about the Lord Jesus, reading the Holy Bible and praying.

About three years later in 303 AD, the Roman emperors Diocletian and Maximian issued their decree written against the Christians. It stated that everyone who lived in the empire must worship the Roman gods, Apollo and Artemis. The Christians were tortured, since we refused to worship the idols, knowing that Christ is the one true God.

Mena decided to leave the army and devote his life to Christ. He wanted to live as a hermit in the Libyan Desert, as someone who spent all his time with God alone. I wanted to go with him.

"Let me come with you Mena!" I cried.
"Forgive me my beloved sister," he said. "I love you greatly, but I need to be in the desert alone so that I could focus on God."
My comfort was that I knew he would be the reason others got to know God. That was more important to me than having him close by.
He loved the open horizon and the clear sky. He remained there in the desert for the next five years, spending his days and nights in prayer, fasting and contemplation on the word of God.

I always worried over how he would survive in the desert. I later found out that Mena had found two camels to help him prepare the land for farming. I imagine he must have planted date palms and olive trees. As little children, we had watched our mother use the date palms, olives and fruit off other trees to make tea, syrup and cakes. Mena particularly loved the fruit cake.
The camels were very loyal to him. They would even bow their heads at night to greet him before they went to sleep.

One night, when Mena was twenty four years old, he saw a vision of angels crowning the martyrs with shiny crowns. He longed to join them and live with Jesus forever. An angel then began speaking to Mena,
"Blessed Mena, you have been chosen as a soldier of Christ to witness to Him before all people. You will be tortured but God will not leave your side. You will be rewarded with 3 crowns: one for your celibacy, one for your worship in the desert and a third for your martyrdom."

In the morning, Mena remembered the angel's voice and returned to our city, the one he had left a few years earlier. Before hurrying to the governor to declare his faith in Christ and fulfill what was predicted, he came to see me. It is during this time we spent together that I found out the details about his life in the army, how he spent his time in the desert, and the vision he saw.

I still remember the day very clearly. The sun was shining, and I was up early drinking tea and reading the Bible. A loud knock on the door startled me and as I went to open up, Mena rushed in.

Immediately I ran to hug him. We drank some hot tea together and he excitedly told me that he was on his way to see the ruler.

"It was the will of God that I return here," he claimed. "I must be a witness to the glory of God before the governor and the rest of the idol worshippers."

I did not want my brother to see the ruler nor did I want him to leave me again. "Please stay, Mena. We can enjoy living together like old times. Most importantly, we can go to church together and pray each day," I pleaded. "I have missed you greatly. Why don't we encourage each other in worshipping God and spreading His word?" But Mena, with tears in his eyes and a large smile, only shook his head and replied, "Sister, I must fulfil the will of God and witness to Him. God will look after you."

"What do you mean?" I asked in return. "What are you planning to do?"
"I heard there is a gathering in the stadium today in celebration of the feast of Apollo, their idol god. Enough of idols! I must show them that Jesus Christ is the only true God," he shouted.
Before I could say anything else, he was off down the street. I scrambled to find a scarf and hurry after him. How exactly was he going to witness to the Lord?

Mena ran into the stadium and out onto the field. Out of breath, I was nearing the stadium when I heard my brother's strong voice, "Enough of this idol worship! These idols are made by hands. Come believe in the one true God, Jesus Christ. He is the One who created you, loves you and died for you!"

I then heard someone else yelling. I turned and found the emperor standing and pointing at Mena. He demanded, "Guards! Go down to the field at once. Have this young man denounce the name of Jesus and worship our idols!"

The guards did as they were told and went down to the field to convince Mena.
"You look familiar. Aren't you Mena, the son of Eudoxius?" One guard asked.
"Surely you will agree to confess that you believe in our idols, Apollo and Artemis. Forget about Jesus Christ."
Mena, however, would not confess. He began to pray and shout, "No, sir. I will not betray the Lord Jesus Christ who I believe in and worship!" With the crowd disturbed and shouting, the governor ordered the guards to arrest him and put him in prison overnight.

The next day, Mena was put on trial and questioned about why he ran out into the stadium.

"I am a servant of the Lord Jesus Christ and my desire is to direct everyone to the truth, that He is the one true God!" he shouted.

"Shut your mouth! I warn you Mena, you are a young man and I don't want to torture you. If you worship Apollo, you will be made free," the governor yelled.

He saw the strength and faith of my brother, and insisted that he be tortured until he worshipped the idols. He first demanded that his arms and legs be stretched and tied to four pegs on the ground and that he be whipped until he bled. He was also tied to a rack and his joints pulled. He was then dragged back and forth over sharp pins fastened to the ground. To worsen his pain, his wounds were rubbed with a rough cloth. His body was also heated and burned with flaming torches. Mena was then beaten with sticks, whipped again and slapped and punched until his teeth fell out.

After all this torture, my brother was thrown into prison again. He kept praying to God while in his pain, "Lord, You were crucified on the cross for my sake, strengthen me to endure this pain for Your sake."
The governor became enraged when Mena would not even accept wealth or power in return for renouncing his Christian faith. So, he was tortured even more. Finally, he gave up trying to convince Mena, so he sent him to another ruler in a region close by. I watched from afar as they carried him onto a boat.

Upon arriving at the next region, he was kept in prison where he met and encouraged other Christians who were also awaiting their trials. In the middle of the first night while praying, a bright light filled the prison cell. Christ appeared to him and spoke with Him!

Christ told Mena how pleased He was with him and how much glory awaited him in Paradise once he completes his life on earth. The Lord also told him that he would be the reason many people turn to God.

The next morning, he was put on trial again by the other governor. After also first trying to convince Mena to deny Christ, the torture began again. He was whipped 100 times with leather straps and then they tried to cut his body. However, the iron saw melted in the guards' hands before they could even begin. In frustration, the governor ordered my brother beheaded. With many people watching, they dragged his body outside to the town square. Mena knelt on the ground and raised his eyes upward to God in a prayer of thanksgiving. At peace, he stretched back his neck and his head was chopped off with a sword.

The crowds were amazed at Mena's courage. Many of them, seeing his strong faith and the miracles, began chanting, "We believe in Jesus Christ! We believe!"

The governor hated that many people believed in Christ because of Mena. He was afraid that he would no longer be mighty and powerful. So, to eliminate any memory of Mena, he then ordered the officers to burn his pure body. A fire was made and burned for three days straight, yet Mena's body would not burn.

Some Christian believers put out the fire on the third night. They took Mena's holy head and body and wrapped them inside an aromatic cloth which they then placed inside a large wooden container. When I heard that my brother's martyrdom was complete, I cried for a long time. As I was crying, a woman who was passing by approached me to comfort me. After hearing that I was Mena's sister, she jumped for joy as she explained that she had become a Christian because of my brother!

The words of Christ had come true, that people turned to God because of Mena! I also remembered the vision he had, that he is now crowned with glory in Paradise, to live in joy with Christ forever! I was quickly comforted and began to thank God.

A number of years later, one of Mena's friends, Athan, was made an army commander. The barbarians were attacking the area of Alexandria in Egypt and so he was ordered to bring his troops there to defend the city. He decided to take Mena's body with him to Egypt as a source of blessing and protection in the battle.

They sailed for five days to arrive in Alexandria. The people there heard about the body and so came to receive the blessings of Mena's body. The troops then put the body on a camel and took it with them to fight the Barbarians. Great miracles happened during the battle because of the blessings of Mena's body which they had with them. Sure enough, they won the battle.

Athan and his troops then tried to take the body back home but the camel did not want to move. This was very strange.

They even tried to have other camels carry the body, but none of the camels would move from that place. Athan realised that this must be a sign from God to leave the body in that area.

Athan, being a close friend of Mena, came to see me upon his return from the battle. He told me about the strong protection Mena's body gave them in the battle. My heart rejoiced at the news and I began to glorify the Lord, repeating the words of Psalm 150, "Praise God in all His saints Alleluia!"

A small tomb was built on the spot where the body was. They then placed the body inside and secured it. Athan and his troops then sailed back home amazed at the wonders they had seen.

Mena's tomb quickly became known and everyone was talking about the blessings and miracles it brought. I ran into a boy who told me that his family took him to the tomb because he was crippled from birth and so could not walk. He crawled nearby my brother's tomb and by the next morning, he could walk perfectly!

As we spoke, a shepherd passing by overheard our conversation. "Mena is a great saint! He performed a miracle for me also! I was feeding my sheep in an area of green pasture nearby and I realised that one lamb was severely sick. As I led the flock along the lake, the sick lamb fell to the ground and became covered in sand. However, when I picked the lamb up, it was miraculously healed! That sand was from the ground outside Mena's tomb!"

Many such miracles made my brother known as, "St Mena, the Wonder Worker."

I wanted to see my brother's tomb myself, so I paid some sailors the few coins that I had, and we began sailing to Alexandria.

I arrived at the city and was kindly taken to the tomb by a priest. As we entered, I could not help but cry at the sight of my brother's body.

"Beloved daughter," the priest spoke. "Your brother is now a martyr of Jesus Christ. You should rejoice for him, as he is now in Paradise."

"What is a martyr?" I questioned the priest.

"The martyrs are those that witness to the reality of the one true God, Jesus Christ. They continue to witness, even until bloodshed. Their glory in heaven is very great," he responded.

Comforted by his words, I began to pray, "Dear Lord, thank you for giving my brother the strength to endure this earthly life. Thank you for the three crowns you gave him for his celibacy, solitude in the desert and martyrdom."

I and all the Christian people now have another friend in heaven, St Mena, who will pray for us always!

www.ingramcontent.com/pod-product-compliance
Lightning Source LLC
Chambersburg PA
CBHW081544090426
42743CB00014BA/3136